CHIEF EXECUTIVES IN BLACK AFRICA AND SOUTHEAST ASIA:
A Descriptive Analysis of Social
Background Characteristics

CHIEF EXECUTIVES IN BLACK AFRICA AND SOUTHEAST ASIA:

A Descriptive Analysis of Social

Background Characteristics

by

Edward Baum

and

Felix Gagliano

Ohio University
   Center for International Studies
   Papers in International Studies
   Africa Series No. 29
   Southeast Asia Series No. 39

CI
PAIS

ISBN: 0-8214-0310-9

Library of Congress Catalog Card
Number: 76-620039

TABLE OF CONTENTS

ILLUSTRATION

PREFACE

Most scholars of developing areas have focused on a particular country or region. Whether from inclination or necessity, this focus has tended to emphasize the characteristics which make a particular country or region unique. The studies arising from this concentration provide valuable information on the area of specialization but usually fail to illuminate what may be larger or global patterns.

As a preliminary exploration of these larger patterns, Professors Baum and Gagliano in this publication, draw on their regional specializations for data on the chief executives of Black Africa and Southeast Asia. Through computer-assisted statistical analyses, they are able to identify similarities and differences in each region and between the regions. Their findings, more suggestive than conclusive, reveal marked similarities between former colonies of a particular European power irregardless of their geographical locale. They also identify a number of variables (i.e., age and higher education) which tend to distinguish one region from the other.

Their most striking finding is the similarities among leaders who have come to power through military coups. This evidence suggests that hypotheses focusing on the particularities of one country are inadequate to explain phenomena which cross racial, national, colonial, and regional boundaries. While hardly obviating the need for culturally sensitive studies-in-depth, the findings emphasize the need to see the forest as well as the tree.

The companion programs of African and Southeast Asian Studies offered by the Ohio University Center for International Studies have encouraged each of the authors in his regional specialization and have facilitated this collaborative effort beyond the regional confines.

Dr. Edward Baum is the Assistant Dean of Faculties for International Studies and an Associate Professor of Government at Ohio University. Prior to his present position, he served as the Director of the African Language and Area Center of Ohio University and earlier spent four years as Head of the Department of History at Advanced Teachers College, Kano, Nigeria as part of the Ohio University/USAID team in Nigeria. He did his Ph.D. work at U.C.L.A. Dr. Felix Gagliano is an Associate Professor of Government and a member of the Southeast Asia Program at Ohio University. He has done considerable fieldwork in Malaysia and is engaged in research there during the present year in association with the Institut Teknoloji MARA. His Ph.D. is from the University of Illinois.

Paul W. van der Veur
Director of Publications
Center for International Studies

May 14, 1976

CHIEF EXECUTIVES IN BLACK AFRICA AND SOUTHEAST ASIA:
A Descriptive Analysis of Social
Background Characteristics

I. *Introduction*

The purpose of this study is to analyze and compare the social background characteristics of the chief executives of Black Africa and Southeast Asia. Scholars from Weber, Pareto, Mosca and Michels, to more recent and systematic writers such as Harold Lasswell, Lester Seligman and Donald Matthews, have established that systematic analysis of the background of those who wield political power is a necessary first step in understanding the social systems in which they operate. From the pens of these and other scholars, an impressive body of social science literature has emerged.[1]

Social backgrounds provide information on the political socialization and recruitment processes. Styles of political recruitment can be differentiated and career patterns unfolded. Other characteristics, such as ethnic background, age, religion, educational background, past positions, and organizational memberships, supply clues to the experience, training, and value orientations of the political leaders. By comparing leaders over time conclusions can be reached about the process, rate, and direction of change. The frequency with which representatives of new groups penetrate the elite is

---

[1]See Carl Beck, James M. Malloy and William R. Campbell, *A Survey of Elite Studies* (Special Operations Office, The American University, 1965); George T. Force and Jack R. Van Der Silk, *Theory and Research in the Study of Political Leadership: An Annotated Bibliography* (Carbondale, 1969); and Harold D. Lasswell, *et. al.*, *The Comparative Study of Elites: An Introduction and Bibliography* (Stanford, 1952), p. 1.

a gauge of the continuity, stability, and restrictiveness of leadership.

The concept "elite" is classificatory and descriptive. Following Lasswell, we agree that "the political elite comprises the top power holders of a body politic."[2] Power holders are those who share in the making of severely sanctioned decisions. Despite the possibility that key political decisions are not always made by office holders, . . ."since the true decision makers are not always known at the beginning of research, the investigator can select government in the conventional sense as a convenient starting point."[3] While it is of great interest to political scientists to establish actual as opposed to formal loci of power,[4] it should be emphasized that the backgrounds of formal office holders offer rich insights into the political process in and of themselves.

For purposes of this study we have assumed that the position of chief executive is the most important political post in each country and that the career patterns and social backgrounds of those who hold that position represents societal expectations of political elites. That is, the chief executive is representative of political elites in the country in general.

Little of the huge leadership literature focuses upon Africa and Asia. There are a few excellent studies of elites

[2]Lasswell, p. 13. For a discussion and schematic presentation of other definitions see Lewis J. Edinger, ed., *Political Leadership in Industrial Societies: Studies in Comparative Analyses* (New York, 1967), pp. 4-9.

[3]Lasswell, p. 8.

[4]Of the several methods of establishing whether such a divergence exists, and if so, of distinguishing between formal and actual holders of power, the "reputational" method is perhaps most widely used. For a description and application example of the procedure see, G. William Skinner, *Leadership and Power in the Chinese Community in Thailand* (Ithaca, 1958).

within individual countries,[5] and a number of political biographies of "charismatic" leaders.[6] It is also true that impressionistic generalizations about leaders of Black Africa and Southeast Asia, and about the leaders of the developing areas are plentiful. Still, little macro-analytic cross-national elite research for these areas has been undertaken.[7]

While our colleagues who specialize in other world areas are doing highly sophisticated leadership studies, probing deeply into leadership at national, state, and local levels, the authors of this study discover that there has been almost no systematic inventory of social background characteristics of the men holding the very highest offices in the nations of Black Africa and Southeast Asia. Even the most elementary demographic attributes of chief executives such as, birthdate, ethnic origin, birthplace, social class, religion, formal education, etc., have not been assembled and systematically studied and compared. This paper addresses itself to this research hiatus. Leadership studies on Black Africa and Southeast Asia are in their infancy.

---

[5]See for example, Patrick J. McGowan and Patrick Bolland, *The Political and Social Elite of Tanzania: An Analysis of Social Background Factors* (Syracuse, 1971). See also, Raymond F. Hopkins, *Political Roles in a New State: Tanzania's First Decade* (New Haven, 1971).

[6]A superb example is Richard Butwell's *U Nu of Burma* (Stanford, 1963). See also, Jean Lacouture, *The Demigods: Charismatic Leadership in the Third World* (New York, 1970).

[7]Important exceptions are summarized for Africa in P.C. Lloyd, ed., *The New Elites of Tropical Africa* (London, 1966). Useful information about leaders in Africa is found in Victor T. Le Vine, *Leadership Transition in Black Africa: Elite Generations and Political Succession*, Munger Africana Library Notes No. 30 (Pasadena, California, 1975). Systematic study of Southeast Asian leadership is more sparse. See however, Fred von der Mehden, *Politics of the Developing Nations* (Englewood Cliffs, 1964), pp. 77-96.

Compilation and analysis of social background inventories is primarily a descriptive process. It is the essential pre-requisite to the theoretically more interesting process of cross-national explanatory analysis of the linkages between social backgrounds and political attitudes and behavior.[8] We accept the premise that social backgrounds are worth gathering primarily for use in establishing these connections.[9] The authors are engaged in a broader project aimed at specifying these linkages among Asian and African leaders.[10] The present paper is a report on the essential first stage of such a study -- the compilation and analysis of social background factors.

II. *Research Parameters*

This study provides background summaries of 115 chief executives of Black Africa and Southeast Asia who held that position between January 1, 1958 and December 31, 1973. It also examines the level of association of background character-istics with region, with major colonial power, and with the recency of the leader.

Southeast Asia is defined conventionally as the ten countries of Indonesia, Singapore, Malaysia, the Philippines, Laos, Cambodia, Burma, Thailand, North and South Vietnam.

---

[8] See for example Carl Beck, *et. al.*, *Comparative Communist Political Leadership* (New York, 1973); and Loch Johnson, "Operational Codes and the Prediction of Leadership Behavior: Senator Frank Church at Mid-Career," paper presented to the American Political Science Association Annual Meeting, New Orleans, September 4-8, 1973.

[9] Lewis J. Edinger and Donald D. Searing, "Social Background in Elite Analysis: A Methodological Inquiry," *American Political Science Review*, LXI (June 1967): 428-445.

[10] The authors plan to use an adapted version of the research design developed by Robert Blackwell for the larger project. See Robert E. Blackwell, Jr., "The Relationship Between Social Background Characteristics, Career Specialization, Political Attitudes and Political Behavior Among Soviet Elites: A Research Design," paper presented at the American Political Science Association Annual Meeting, New Orleans, September 4-8, 1973.

Black Africa refers to those 35 "sovereign states. . .
governed by black people."[11] (See Appendix A for a list
of the leaders and their countries.) Chief executive
refers to the functional head of government rather than
a ceremonial Chief of State. The time period, January 1,
1958 to December 31, 1973, was chosen to provide a common
time frame for leaders of independent African and Southeast Asian countries.

The information categories used are a considerably
adapted version of those outlined by Harold D. Lasswell.[12]
Our interest in this stage of the project was confined to
background summaries and basic associations controlling
for region, major colonial power, and first vs. current
leader.

III. *The Findings*

Decade of Birth (Table 1).[13] The chief executives in
this study were born in a period ranging from 1891 to 1941.
For all leaders the median year of birth is 1918 with over
half born between 1910 and 1920. While there is almost no
association between former major colonial power and decade
of birth (Cramer's V of .218), there is a mild association
between continent and birth decade (V=.305).[14] This may
be explained, in part, by the relative youth of many of
the new military leaders of Africa compared with military
leaders of Southeast Asia. Over a decade separates the

---

[11]Donald Morrison, *et. al.*, *Black Africa: A Comparative
Handbook* (New York, 1972), p. XXVI. We have included two
countries which have become independent since 1968 but which
were not part of the Black Africa study, Equatorial Guinea
and Swaziland.   We have also included the Malagasy Republic.

[12]Lasswell, *passim.*

[13]Tables are included in Appendix B.

[14]Cramer's V and other statistical tools are defined
in Appendix B, page 25.

ages of the military leaders of the two continents (Southeast
Asia mean birth year is 1915+ while in Black Africa it is
1928+; the range for military leaders in Southeast Asia is
1897-1930, while for Africa it is 1909-1940). This in part
is a reflection of the relative recency of the Africanization
of the military. Generally speaking, however, Asian and
African leaders are fairly young.[15]

Social Origins (Table 2). Chief executives tend to be
from families with high social status, either traditional elite
or other upper class position. This holds true of both Africa
and Southeast Asia. Over 50% of the leaders fall into these
categories. While there appears no significant association
with continent (Cramer's V of .060) there is a weak association
with former colonial power (V=.217). Among former French
Colonies, 65% of the chief executives for whom we have data
come from families with high social status. This finding is
somewhat surprising in view of the conventional opinion that
the British rather than the French developed cadres of high
status leaders in their colonies.

Size of Place of Rearing (Table 3). Over a third of the
leaders spent their youth in towns or cities of at least
10,000 population -- a much higher proportion than that of the
total population in Africa and Southeast Asia before World War
II. Controlling for major colonial power produces no association (V=.179). When controlling for first or current leader
there is a slightly higher proportion of current leaders who
are from small towns (V=.234). When dividing by continent,
V rises to .599. There is an absence of African leaders
from towns between 5,000 and 10,000 population. It is interesting to note that of the 11 leaders who have been the only

---

[15]See page 11 for a discussion of age upon becoming chief
executive.

leaders of their country between 1958 and 1973, 90.9% are from towns under 5,000 population.

Religion (Table 4). The impact of the colonial era is evident in that almost half of the chief executives were Christian (Protestant 17.3%, Catholic 26.7%). There is a noticeable difference between the continents. Christianity accounts for 58% of African leaders, but only 19% of Asian leaders (Cramer's V = .723). This is undoubtedly due to the longer tradition of competing organized large-scale religions in Southeast Asia (Buddhism and Islam) as compared with Black Africa. Dichotomizing between Christian and non-Christian, we find a Yule's Q of association of .722 with continent as the independent variable.[16] There is a strong association between religion and major colonial power (Cramer's V = .501). There is almost no association between first and current leaders and Christianity (V=.157).

Formal Education (Table 5). There is a relatively high degree of formal education among these leaders, with 47% receiving at least some university level education. There is a mild association between continent and level of education (V=.410) and between major colonial power and education (V=.405). Thus, a higher proportion of the leaders in Southeast Asia than those in Black Africa had some university education. Also leaders from former British areas are more likely to have attended a university than those from former French areas. The strength of higher education among Southeast Asian leaders arises, in part, out of the longer tradition of university level education in that area of the world. There has been some slight shift away from university education between first and

---

[16] Yule's Q is defined in Appendix B, page 25.

current leaders (44% to 37.5%) but the association between
first and current and education is not strong (V=.252).

With respect to *location of education* (Table 6) almost
half of the leaders studied abroad, usually, but not ex-
clusively, in the mother country. There are minimal associations between continent (V=.291) and major colonial power
(V=.317) with location of education. Only one (2.9%) of the
leaders with British colonial background for whom we have
data studied in another country without also studying in
Britain, whereas six (13.6%) of the leaders with French
background who studied abroad did not also study in France.
Or, of the leaders who studied abroad, among the former
British colonies, 97% had some of their education in
Britain, whereas among the French, 75% studied in France.

Prime Occupation (Table 7). Analysis of the prime
occupations of chief executives confirms the importance of
administrative or bureaucratic positions, particularly the
armed forces (30%), educators (17%), and the civil service
(10%), as stepping stones to the most important political
position of each country. This can be explained partly by
the nature of colonial administration in which most of the
new positions available to educated Africans, and to a less
extent, Asians, were with the colonial bureaucracy. It is
also due to the large number of army officers who have taken
control of various countries in these two continents. Indeed,
in Africa, in all but two instances where the independence
leader was not the chief executive in December, 1973, the
chief executive was a military officer. In the two exceptions,
Liberia and Gabon, the present chief executive was vice-
president when the former leaders, W.V.S. Tubman and Leon
M'Ba, respectively, died.

There are some important differences between continents,
between colonial power, and between first and last leaders.

In Africa educators form the second largest occupational
group, with 20% of the total (30% of the non-military
leaders whose occupation is known). Educators form only
7% of the chief executives in Southeast Asia. In Southeast Asia the largest non-military group consists of
lawyers (24% of the total, 37% of the non-military leaders).
In Africa lawyers account for 7% of the leaders. This is
partly explained by the existence of teaching as the only
acceptable alternative to many who received secondary or
university education. Cramer's V is .358 for occupation
controlling for continent.

The importance of lawyers among British colonies may
be noted by the 20% of chief executives who were lawyers,
compared with 2% among former French colonies. On the
other hand, civil servants account for 10% of former
French chief executives, but none among the former British
colonies, (Cramer's V = .485).

As is well known, there is a tremendous shift in
occupations between first and current leaders. Whereas
only one of the independence leaders was a military man,
of current leaders in countries where there has been a
change, 73% are soldiers. The six non-military chief
executives in these latter countries are spread among
education (1), civil service (2), commerce (1), and
law (3) (V=.759).

Early Political or Public Experience (Table 8).
There appear two major paths to the post of chief executive:
through a political career involving party activity leading
to legislative involvement and cabinet membership, or
through the armed forces (see below). Among the first
leaders in countries in which there has been a change 35%
(8) began their public career in a political party post
and 26% (6) in the civil service. Among current leaders

64% (14) started in the military. Among the 14 persons who have been in power throughout this period, only 1 (6%) began in a party post even though 36% (5) started as elected officials. Perhaps "non-partisan" leaders have better hopes of a long tenure.

The age of this *first political or public experience* (Table 9) is fairly young. Among career military officers, it is very young. Of the 24 military men for whom we have data, 83% entered the army by age 24 (42% by age 19). But for the non-military leaders the median age was 29. As Table 9 indicates, there is a slight difference between continents. The median age group for African leaders was 30-34, while among Southeast Asian leaders it is 25-29.

Political Party Experience (Table 10). In only two cases, both in Southeast Asia, did a military leader have political party experience prior to assuming the position as chief executive. Southeast Asian non-military leaders were more likely to have extensive party experience (75% with six or more years compared with 59% for African leaders). Leaders from former British colonies were also more likely to have extensive party experience (74% compared with 64% for former French colonies).

Legislative Experience (Table 11). Only one military leader had any legislative experience. Of the non-military leaders over a third (39% had a minimum of 6 years legislative experience. Non-military leaders of Southeast Asia were more likely to have extensive legislative experience (60% vs. 33% for Black Africa) partly as a result of the shorter period of time during which legislatures have been in operation in Africa. Between former British and French colonies there is relatively little difference (extensive experience in British, 37%, in French 33%).

Cabinet Experience (Table 12). Whereas legislative and party experience are both normal characteristics of non-military political leaders, this is not necessarily true of cabinet experience. Indeed, 35% of these leaders possessed no cabinet experience, and only 21% had extensive cabinet experience. There is a minimal association between continent and cabinet experience (V=.144) and weak association with major colonial power (V=.229).

Paths to the Chief Executive's Office. There appear to be two main "paths" to the top political position which have been followed by the leaders in this study. The most obvious, given the normal workings of parliamentary democracy, is through the legislature, to the cabinet, to either the post of prime minister or president. The second "path" is, of course, through the military, although it is highly unlikely that many of the persons who entered the military originally considered this to be a path to political success. Eighty percent of the non-military chief executives had some legislative experience, and over 60% possessed some cabinet experience. Of the non-military leaders, for whom we have data, 60% (36) had either had cabinet experience or had served as deputy prime minister or the equivalent.

Age Upon Becoming Chief Executive (Table 13). The leaders of Black Africa and Southeast Asia have been fairly young when they assumed the position of chief executive for the first time with the median and the mode being in the 40-49 years old category. There has been a slight shift between first and current leaders, with the 30-39 age group increasing from 20% to 28% of the leaders while the 50-59 age group has declined from 28% to 16%. As Table 13 indicates, there are weak associations with continent (V=.280), with major colonial power (V=.185), and with first and current leaders (V=.318).

Means of Becoming Chief Executive (Table 14). The majority of all leaders came to power through constitutional means, either regular constitutional transfer (59%) or through hereditary succession (2%); a third achieved the top position through a coup d'état. Over two-thirds of current leaders have forceably taken over the position as chief executive. Thus, Cramer's V for first vs. current leaders is .706. Association between continent or former colonial power is either negligible or weak (for continent V=.114, for Britain/France V=.181).

Total Tenure as Chief Executive (Table 15). The total time these leaders have served as chief executive has averaged 5 years 1 month. This does not compare unfavorably with such countries as the United States which is barely over five years, or Great Britain which, since 1886, has averaged four years ten months per prime minister. However, the distribution of tenure is bi-modal, with 20% having served terms of less than one year, and 25% serving nine years or longer. Table 15 indicates average tenure of chief executive, while Chart A shows the distribution.

IV. *Conclusion*

The most striking feature of this comparison of African and Southeast Asian leaders is the similarity of their social backgrounds. Although as noted, African leaders are somewhat younger and Southeast Asian leaders have a somewhat higher level of formal education, their essential similarity over time is remarkable.

Another notable feature emerging from our data is the relative degree of executive stability characteristic of both regions, although when a transfer of power has occured it has usually been by force. The frequency of military coups suggests that political succession is highly problematic in both areas.

The basic trend noted is the growing number of military leaders in Africa and Southeast Asia. Military leaders now are in power in 44% of the nations of Black Africa and Southeast Asia. They differ significantly from the civilian leaders they displaced by force. Seventy-three percent are from lower or middle class origins as opposed to 40% of the civilians. Military leaders tend to be younger as well; 72% were born since 1920 as compared to 44% of the civilians. More military men came from small towns (60%) than did their civilian rivals (55%). They tend to be less well educated; only 34% had university training compared to 52% of the civilians. They have virtually no experience in political parties or the legislature. A notable difference between African and Asian military leaders is the extent of foreign travel experience of the former. Seventy-five percent of African military leaders studied abroad (compared with 43% of African civilian leaders), while only 33.3% of the Southeast Asian military leaders studied abroad (contrast 66.7% of Asian civilian leaders).

The rise of the military suggests an increasing reliance upon force and the "strategy of intimidation,"[17] for gaining, keeping, and changing chief executive positions in these regions, as well as the fragility of the essentially European executive structures transplanted to African and Asian soil.

Perhaps of greater importance is the point that the trend toward chief-executives-in-uniform swept Africa and Southeast Asia at approximately the same time, in a much tighter time period than did the forces of nationalism and independence. Some scholars have recently suggested that the coherence of experience in "the developing areas" has declined so markedly as to make it more logical to study individual national experiences rather than regional or conceptual collectivities.

---

[17]Howard Wriggins, *The Ruler's Imperative: Strategies for Political Survival in Asia and Africa* (New York, 1969).

Our data tentativly suggests that a broad focus may still have logic. Despite the diversity in their cultures, colonial backgrounds, and independence dates, Asia and Africa seem to be reacting in common to contemporary forces, giving them greater similarity than we might have hertofore grasped.

These hypotheses need more investigation. The authors hope to bring additional evidence to bear upon the phenomenon of leadership in Africa and Southeast Asia in the next stage of this research project.

FIGURE I

SUMMARY PROFILE OF LEADERS*

CHARACTERISTICS	Total Profile	Profile by Continent		Profile by Major Col. Pow.		Profile of First vs. Recent	
		Africa	S.E. Asia	Britain	France	First	First Dec. 73
	(n=115)	(n=85)	(n=30)	(n=35)	(n=50)	(n=26)	(n=26)
BACKGROUND ATTRIBUTES							
Median Birth Year...	1918	1919	1912			1909	1922
Parents' Soc. Class...	Upper (56%)						
Town of Rearing...	Under 10,000 (54%)	Under 5,000 (53%)					
Religion...	Christian (44%)		Buddhist (48%)		Varies		Varies
Education...	Secondary (49%)		University (77%)	University (74%)			
Study Abroad?...	No (52%)		Yes (58%)	Yes (68%)			
*CAREER ATTRIBUTES***							
Prime Occupation...	Educ. or Law (42%)	Educ. or Civ. Serv. (47%)	Law or Politics (53%)		Educ. or Civ. Serv. (32%)		
First Public Post...	Party Post or Civ. Serv. (59%)	Civ. Serv. or Elect. (60%)	Party Post or Civ. Serv. (75%)				
Age Entered Public Life...	Betw. 25-34 (50%)		Before 29 (53%)				
High Post Before CE.	Cabinet Level 60%						
Legislative Exp...	3+ years (57%)		6+ years (57%)			1+ years (55%)	6+ years (67%)
Cabinet Exp...	1 or more years (56%)					Under 1 yr. (57%)	
CHIEF EXECUTIVE ATTRIBUTES							
Age When Became CE..	By age 49 (62%)						
Mean Tenure...	About 5 years					About 8 yrs.	
Means of Attaining Post...	Constitu-tionally (64%)						Coup d'état (69%)

*Characteristics for Continent, Major Power, or Recent Leaders are indicated only when they differ from the total profile.

**Non-military leaders excluded from this attribute.

Summary of Countries and Leaders Since
Independence or World War II[@]

FORMER COLONIAL POWER	FORMER COLONIAL POWER
State (Independence)	*State* (Independence)
Leaders (Term[s])	Leaders (Term[s])

AFRICA	ASIA
NONE	*NONE*
Ethiopia (Early Times)	*Thailand* (Early Times)
Haile Selassie (11/ 2/30 - 9/12/74)	Khuang Aphaiwong[@] (8/ 1/44 - 8/17/45) (1/31/46 - 3/18/46) (11/10/47 - 4/ 8/48)[1]
Liberia (July 26, 1847)	Thawee Bunyaket[@] (8/31/45 - 9/16/45)
William V.S. Tubman (5/ 6/43 - 7/23/71)	Seni Pramoj[@] (9/17/45 - 1/30/46)
William R. Tolbert (7/23/71 -)	Pridi Phanomyong[@] (3/24/46 - 8/23/46)
	Dhamrong Navaswat[@] (8/23/46 - 11/ 9/47)
	Phiboon Songkram[@1] (12/16/38 - 8/ 1/44) (4/ 8/48 - 9/16/57)
	Pote Sarasin[@] (9/21/57 - 12/26/57)
	Thanom Kittikachorn (1/ 1/58 - 10/20/58) (12/ 9/63 - 10/15/73)
	Sarit Dhanaratja (2/ 9/59 - 12/ 8/63)
	Sanya Thammasakdi (10/15/73 - 2/15/75)

AFRICA	ASIA
BRITAIN	*BRITAIN*
Botswana (Sept. 30, 1966)	*Burma* (Jan. 4, 1948)
Seretse Khama	U Nu
(9/30/66 -)	(1/ 2/48 - 6/ 5/56)
Gambia (Feb. 18, 1965)	(2/24/57 - 10/29/58)
Dauda Jawara	(2/ 6/60 - 3/ 2/62)
(6/ 1/62 -)	Ba Swee[@]
Ghana (March 6, 1957)	(6/ 5/56 - 2/24/57)
Kwame Nkrumah	Ne Win
(3/ 5/52 - 2/24/66)	(10/29/58 - 2/ 6/60)
Joseph Ankrah	(3/ 2/62 -)
(2/24/66 - 4/ 2/69)	*Malaysia* (Sept. 16, 1963)[2]
A.A. Afrifa	Abdul Rahman
(4/ 2/69 - 9/ 3/69)	(7/27/55 - 9/21/70)
Kofi Busia	Abdul Razak
(9/ 3/69 - 1/13/72)	(9/21/70 - 1/14/76)
Ignatius Acheampong	*Singapore* (August 9, 1965)
(1/13/72 -)	Lee Kuan Yew
Kenya (Dec. 12, 1963)	(6/ 5/59 -)
Jomo Kenyatta	
(6/ 1/63 -)	
Lesotho (Oct. 4, 1966)	
Leabua Jonathan'	
(7/ 7/65 -)	
Malawi (July 6, 1964)	
H. Kamuzu Banda	
(2/ 1/63 -)	
Nigeria (Oct. 1, 1960)	
Abubakar Tafawa Balewa	
(8/30/57 - 1/15/66)	
Johnson Aguiyi-Ironsi	
(1/16/66 - 7/29/66)	
Yakubu Gowon	
(7/29/66 - 7/29/75)	

AFRICA	ASIA

BRITAIN (cont.)

  Sierra Leone (April 27, 1961)

    Milton Margai
      (7/ 9/54 - 4/28/64)

    Albert Margai
      (5/ 1/64 - 3/24/67)

    Andrew Juxom-Smith
      (3/24/67 - 4/18/68)

    Siaka Stevens
      (4/26/68 -   )

  Sudan (Jan. 1, 1956)

    Ishmail el-Azhari[@]
      (1/ 1/56 - 7/ 4/56)

    Adballah Khalil
      (7/ 5/56 - 11/17/58)

    Ibrahim Abboud
      (11/17/58 - 10/30/64)

    el-Khatim el-Khalifah
      (10/30/64 - 6/10/65)

    Muhommed Mahgoub
      (6/10/65 - 7/25/66)
      (5/18/67 - 5/25/69)

    Sayed Siddik El Mahdi
      (7/31/66 - 5/15/67)

    Abubakr Awadallah
      (5/25/69 - 10/28/69)

    Gaafar al Nimeiry
      (10/28/69 -   )

  Swaziland (Sept. 6, 1968)

    Sobhuza II
      (/ /21 -   )

  Tanzania (Dec. 9, 1961)

    Julius Nyerere
      (9/ 2/60 -   )[3]

AFRICA	ASIA
BRITAIN (cont.)	
Uganda (Oct. 9, 1962)	
Apollo Milton Obote (4/30/62 - 1/25/71)	
Idi Amin (1/25/71 -)	
Zambia (Oct. 24, 1964)	
Kenneth Kaunda (1/22/64 -)	

AFRICA	ASIA
FRANCE	*FRANCE*
Cameroon (Jan. 1, 1960)	*Cambodia* (Dec. 29, 1954)
Ahmadou Ahidjo (2/18/58 -)	Norodom Sihanouk (4/26/41 - 3/18/70)
Central African Republic (August 13, 1960)	Lon Nol (3/18/70 - 4/ 1/75)
David Dacko (4/30/59 - 1/ 1/66)	*Laos* (Dec. 29, 1954)[4]
Jean-Bedel Bokassa (1/ 1/66 -)	Katay Sasorith[@] (8/18/54 - 12/25/56)
Chad (Aug. 11, 1960)	Souvanna Phouma (3/22/56 - 8/ 5/58) (8/ 9/60 - 12/16/60) (8/23/62 - 11/29/75)
Francois Tombalbaye (3/24/59 - 4/13/75)	Phoui Sananikone (8/16/58 - 12/30/59)
Congo (Aug. 15, 1960)	Kou Abhay (1/ 7/60 - 5/30/60)
Fulbert Youlou (11/21/59 - 8/15/63)	Tiao Somsanith (6/ 1/60 - 8/ 9/60)
Alphonse Massemba-Debat (12/19/63 - 8/ 4/68)	Bon Oum (12/16/60 - 6/11/62)
Alfred Raoul (9/ 4/68 - 1/ 1/69)	*North Viet Nam* (Sept. 2, 1945)
Marien Ngoubi (1/ 1/69 -)	Ho Chi Minh (9/ 2/45 - 9/ 3/69)
Dahomey (Aug. 1, 1960)[5]	Pham Van Dong (9/ 3/69 -)
Hubert Maga (5/18/59 - 10/29/63) (5/ 7/70 - 5/ 7/72)	

AFRICA	ASIA

FRANCE (cont.)

  Dahomey (cont.)

    Christophe Soglo
      (10/29/63 - 1/25/64)
      (12/22/65 - 12/17/67)

    Sourou Migan Apithy
      (1/25/64 - 11/29/65)

    Alphonse Alley
      (12/17/67 - 7/17/68)

    Emile-Derin Zinsou
      (7/17/68 - 12/10/69)

    Paul Emile de Souza
      (12/13/69 - 5/ 7/70)

    Justin Ahomadegbe
      (5/ 7/72 - 10/ /72)

    Mathieu Kerekou
      (10/ /72 -)

  Gabon (Aug. 17, 1960)

    Leon M'Ba
      (12/24/57 - 11/28/69)

    Albert-Bernard Bongo
      (11/28/69 -)

  Guinea (Oct. 2, 1958)

    Sekou Toure
      (10/ 2/58 -)

  Ivory Coast (Aug. 7, 1960)

    Felix Houphouet-Boigny
      (5/ 1/59 -)

  Malagasy Republic (June 26, 1960)

    Philibert Tsiranana
      (5/ 1/59 - 5/18/72)

    Gabriel Ramanantsoa
      (5/18/72 - 2/ 5/75)

  Mali (Sept. 22, 1960)

    Modibo Keita
      (4/ 4/59 - 11/19/68)

    Moussa Traore
      (11/19/68 -)

FRANCE (cont.)

  South Viet Nam (Dec. 29, 1954)

    Ngo Dinh Diem
      (10/23/55 - 11/ 1/63)

    Duong Van Minh
      (11/ 1/63 - 1/30/64)

    Nguyen Khanh
      (1/30/64 - 10/25/64)

    Tran Van Hung
      (10/26/64 - 1/26/65)

    Nguyen Xuan Oanh[@6]
      (1/27/65 - 2/15/65)

    Phan Huy Quat
      (2/16/65 - 6/11/65)

    Nguyen Cao Ky
      (6/19/65 - 9/ 3/67)

    Nguyen Van Thieu
      (9/ 3/67 - 4/21/75)

AFRICA	ASIA
FRANCE (cont.)	
Mauritania (Nov. 1, 1960)	
Mokhtar Ould Daddah (6 /24 /59 -)	
Niger (Sept. 3, 1960)	
Hamani Diori (12/14/58 - 4/15/74)	
Senegal (Aug. 20, 1960)	
Leopold Sedar Senghor (9/ 5/60 -)	
Togo (April 27, 1960) [7]	
Sylvanus Olympio (5/16/58 - 1/13/63)	
Nicholas Grunitsky (1/13/63 - 1/13/67)	
Etienne Eyadema (4/14/67 -)	
Upper Volta (Aug. 5, 1960)	
Maurice Yameogo (4/27/59 - 4/ 3/66)	
Sangoule Lamizana (1/ 3/66 -)	
SPAIN	
Equatorial Guinea (Oct. 12, 1968)	
Francisco Macias-Nguema (9/22/68 -)	
BELGIUM	
Burundi (July 1, 1962) [8]	
Andre Muhirwa (7/ 1/62 - 6/10/63)	

Pierre Ngendandumwe
    (6/17/63 - 4/ 1/64)
    (1/12/65 - 1/15/65)	

Albin Nyamoya (4/ 1/64 - 1/ 7/65)	

AFRICA	ASIA
BELGIUM (cont.)	
Burundi (cont.)	
Joseph Bamina	
(1/24/65 - 4/ 1/65)	
Leopold Biha	
(9/13/65 - 7/ 8/66)	
Michael Micombero	
(7/ 8/66 -)	
Rwanda (July 1, 1962)	
Greogoire Kayibanda	
(10/ 9/61 - 7/ 5/73)	
Juvenal Habyarimana	
(7/ 5/73 -)	
Zaire (June 30, 1960) [9]	
Patrice Lumumba	
(6/30/60 - 9/ 5/60)	
Joseph Ileo	
(9/ 5/60 - 9/30/60)	
(2/ 9/61 - 8/16/61)	
Cyril Adoula	
(8/16/61 - 7/10/64)	
Moise Tshombe	
(7/10/64 - 10/13/65)	
Everiste Kimba	
(10/18/65 - 11/25/65)	
Joseph Mobutu (Mobuto Sese Seko)	
(9/30/60 - 2/ 9/61)	
(11/25/65 -)	
ITALY	
Somalia(July 1, 1960)	
Aden Abdulla Osman	
(7/ 1/60 - 7/ 1/67)	
Abdirashid Ali Shermarke	
(7/ 1/67 - 10/15/69)	
Mohammed Siad Barre	
(10/21/69 -)	

AFRICA	ASIA
	USA
	Phillipines (July 4, 1946)
	Carlos Garcia
	(3/17/57 - 1/ 1/62)
	Diosdado Macapagal
	(1/ 1/62 - 1/ 1/66)
	Ferdinand E. Marcos
	(1/ 1/66 -)

AFRICA	ASIA
	NETHERLANDS
	Indonesia (Aug. 17, 1945)
	Sukarno
	(8/17/45 - 11/13/45)
	(7/ 5/59 - 3/11/66)
	Sutan Sjahrir@
	(11/14/45 - 6/27/47)
	Amir Sjarifuddin@
	(7/ 3/47 - 1/23/48)
	Mohammed Hatta@
	(1/29/48 - 9/ 6/50)
	Mohammed Natsir@
	(9/ 6/50 - 4/27/51)
	Sukiman Wirjosanjojo@
	(4/27/51 - 4/ 3/52)
	Wilopo@
	(4/ 1/52 - 8/ 1/53)
	Ali Sastroamidjojo@
	(8/ 1/53 - 9/12/55)
	(3/26/56 - 4/19/57)
	Burhanuddin Harahap@
	(8/12/55 - 3/26/56)
	Djuanda Kartawidjojo
	(3/ 8/57 - 7/ 5/59)
	Suharto
	(3/11/66 -)

@Leaders with an @ after their name served before 1958 and are not included in this study but are listed here for information.

[1]Phiboon Songkram headed a military clique which controlled the government after November 10, 1947.

[2]Malaya, the largest constituent unit in Malaysia, became independent on August 31, 1957.

[3]Julius Nyerere was not in office between January and November 1962, but for purposes of this study was assumed to have been.

[4]The political situation in Laos was quite confused during the period 1958-1962.

[5]Christophe Soglo established a provisional government between November 29, 1965 and December 22, 1965, whose head was Tahirou Congacou, but real control was in the hands of Soglo.

[6]Acting Premier appointed by Nguyen Khanh.

[7]Between January and April, 1967, a Committee of National Reconciliation was responsible for the government.

[8]Pie Masumbuko was Acting Premier, January 15-24, and is not included in this study.

[9]Between September, 1960, and February, 1961, government was the responsibility of a College of Commissioners established by Joseph Mobutu who is, therefore, listed as having power during this period.

Summary of numbers of countries and (leaders included in study by continent and former colonial power:

Col.Pow.	None	Britain	France	Spain	Belg	USA	Italy	Neth	Total
Cont.: Africa	2(3)	13(30)	15(34)	1(1)	3(14)		1(3)		35(85)
Asia	1(3)	3(5)	4(16)			1(3)		1(3)	10(30)
	3(6)	16(35)	19(50)	1(1)	3(14)	1(3)	1(3)	1(3)	45(115)

Tables of Characteristics

Each table provides frequencies of each category and cross-tabulations by Continent (Africa/Asia), Former Major Colonial Power (Britain/France), and Relative Recency of Term of Office (First/Current, Dec. 1973). The two measures of association used are Cramer's V and Contingency Coefficient (C), as determined by the Statistical Package for the Social Sciences (SPSS). Cramer's V is a chi-square based measure of association which varies between 0.0 and 1.0, with higher numbers indicating stronger association. Contingency Coefficient is also based on chi-square and varies between 0.0 and 1.0. However, for smaller tables (especially those less than 5 x 5) the upper limit is less than 1.0. Because of this a corrected C was computed using the table of divisors in Dean J. Champion, *Basic Statistics for Social Research* (Scranton, Pa., 1970), p. 206. This book also discusses the advantages and disadvantages of each of the measures of association commonly used by social scientists. Some tables also include Yule's Q as a measure of association. Q is computed from 2 x 2 tables and varies between -1.0 and +1.0.

TABLE 1

DECADE OF BIRTH

| Category | ......Continent...... | | ..Former Col. Power.. | | ..First or 73 Leader.. | | All Leaders |
	Africa	S.E. Asia	Britain	France	First/58	Dec. 73	Totals
1890-1899........	7 (8.8)	3 (10.7)	5 (14.3)	2 (4.3)	5 (19.2)	0 (0.0)	10 (9.3)
1900-1909........	12 (15.0)	11 (39.3)	7 (20.0)	12 (25.5)	8 (30.8)	4 (16.7)	23 (21.3)
1910-1919........	24 (30.0)	7 (25.0)	8 (22.9)	16 (34.0)	6 (23.1)	6 (25.0)	31 (28.7)
1920-1929........	20 (25.0)	6 (21.4)	9 (25.7)	9 (19.1)	6 (23.1)	5 (20.8)	26 (24.1)
1930-1939........	15 (18.8)	1 (3.6)	6 (17.1)	8 (17.0)	1 (3.8)	8 (33.3)	16 (14.8)
1940-1949........	2 (2.5)	0 (0.0)	0 (0.0)	0 (0.0)	0 (0.0)	1 (4.2)	2 (1.9)
Totals........	80	28	35	47	26	24	108
Measures							
Cramer's V....	.305		.218		.506		
Cont. Coef....	.292		.213		.452		
Cbar.........	.382		.278		.591		
Missing Data..	7		3		2		7

TABLE 2

PARENT'S SOCIAL CLASS

| Category | ......Continent...... | | ..Former Col. Power.. | | ..First or 73 Leader.. | | All Leaders |
	Africa	S.E. Asia	Britain	France	First/58	Dec. 73	Totals
Trad. Elite......	13 (32.5)	8 (38.1)	9 (39.1)	8 (34.8)	5 (31.3)	3 (30.0)	22 (36.1)
Other Hi Stat...	9 (22.5)	4 (19.0)	3 (13.0)	7 (30.4)	4 (25.0)	3 (30.0)	12 (19.7)
Middle Class....	10 (25.0)	5 (23.8)	6 (26.1)	4 (17.4)	4 (31.3)	1 (10.0)	15 (24.6)
Lower Class.....	8 (20.0)	4 (19.0)	5 (21.7)	4 (17.4)	2 (12.5)	3 (30.0)	12 (19.7)
Totals........	40	21	23	23	15	10	61
Measures							
Cramer's V....	.060		.217		.294		
Cont. Coef....	.060		.212		.282		
Cbar.........	.081		.290		.386		
Missing Data..	54		39		26		54

TABLE 3

SIZE OF PLACE OF REARING

Category	......Continent......		..Former Col. Power..		..First or 73 Leader..		All Leaders
	Africa	S.E. Asia	Britain	France	First/58	Dec. 73	Totals
Under 5,000..	20 (52.6)	3 (18.8)	6 (35.3)	12 (48.0)	7 (43.7)	5 (38.5)	23 (42.6)
5,000-10,000..	0 (0.0)	6 (37.5)	3 (17.6)	2 (8.0)	2 (12.5)	2 (15.4)	6 (11.1)
10,000-50,000..	13 (34.2)	3 (18.8)	6 (35.3)	8 (32.0)	4 (31.3)	4 (30.8)	16 (29.6)
Capital or over 50,000..	3 (7.9)	3 (18.8)	1 (5.9)	2 (8.0)	1 (6.3)	0 (0.0)	6 (11.1)
Other..	2 (5.3)	1 (6.3)	1 (5.9)	1 (4.0)	1 (6.3)	2 (15.4)	3 (2.6)
Totals..	38	16	17	25	15	13	54
Measures							
Cramer's V...	.599		.179		.234		
Cont. Coef...	.514		.176		.228		
Cbar...	.683		.234		.303		
Missing Data.	61		43		23		

TABLE 4

RELIGIOUS BACKGROUND

Category	......Continent......		..Former Col. Power..		..First or 73 Leader..		All Leaders
	Africa	S.E. Asia	Britain	France	First/58	Dec. 73	Totals
Islam..	14 (29.2)	5 (18.5)	8 (29.6)	5 (17.9)	4 (23.8)	4 (28.6)	19 (25.3)
Buddhism..	0 (0.0)	13 (48.1)	2 (7.4)	8 (28.6)	3 (14.3)	3 (21.4)	13 (17.3)
Protestant..	13 (27.1)	0 (0.0)	9 (33.3)	1 (3.6)	3 (14.3)	2 (14.3)	13 (17.3)
Catholic..	15 (31.3)	5 (18.5)	4 (14.8)	10 (35.7)	8 (38.1)	4 (28.6)	20 (26.7)
Local Relig..	5 (10.4)	0 (0.0)	2 (7.4)	1 (3.6)	0 (0.0)	0 (0.0)	5 (6.7)
No Relig..	1 (2.1)	4 (14.8)	2 (7.4)	3 (10.7)	2 (9.5)	1 (7.1)	5 (6.7)
Totals..	48	27	27	28	20	14	75
Measures							
Cramer's V...	.723		.501		.157		
Cont. Coef...	.586		.448		.155		
Cbar...	.7659		.586		.202		
Missing Data.	40		30		17		

TABLE 5

HIGHEST LEVEL OF FORMAL EDUCATION

Category	......Continent......		..Former Col. Power..		..First or 73 Leader..		All Leaders
	Africa	S.E. Asia	Britain	France	First/58	Dec. 73	Totals
Post-Grad.......	11 (13.6)	13 (50.0)	13 (38.2)	5 (11.1)	6 (24.0)	3 (12.5)	24 (22.4)
University......	19 (23.5)	8 (26.9)	12 (35.3)	11 (24.4)	5 (20.0)	6 (25.0)	26 (24.3)
Secondary......	46 (56.8)	6 (23.1)	8 (23.5)	27 (60.0)	13 (52.0)	14 (58.3)	52 (48.6)
Primary........	4 (4.9)	0 (0.0)	1 (2.9)	2 (4.4)	0 (0.0)	1 (4.2)	4 (3.7)
None..........	1 (1.2)	0 (0.0)	0 (0.0)	0 (0.0)	1 (4.0)	0 (0.0)	1 (.9)
Totals......	81	26	34	45	25	24	107
Measures							
Cramer's V...	.410		.405		.252		
Cont. Coef...	.379		.375		.244		
Cbar........	.504		.499		.324		
Missing Data..	8		6		2		8

TABLE 6

LOCATION OF FORMAL EDUCATION

Category	......Continent......		..Former Col. Power..		..First or 73 Leader..		All Leaders
	Africa	S.E. Asia	Britain	France	First/58	Dec. 73	Totals
Home Cntry. Only	44 (55.7)	11 (42.3)	11 (32.4)	20 (45.5)	16 (61.5)	13 (54.2)	55 (52.4)
Home and Col. Cntry. Only....	26 (32.9)	8 (30.8)	15 (44.1)	16 (36.4)	3 (11.5)	7 (29.2)	34 (32.4)
Another Cntry...	2 (2.5)	5 (19.2)	1 (2.9)	6 (13.6)	4 (15.4)	2 (8.3)	7 (6.7)
Both Col. Cntry. and Another Cntry.........	7 (8.9)	2 (7.7)	7 (20.6)	2 (4.5)	3 (11.5)	2 (8.3)	9 (8.6)
Totals......	79	26	34	44	26	24	105
Measures							
Cramer's V...	.291		.317		.232		
Cont. Coef...	.280		.302		.226		
Cbar........	.384		.414		.310		
Missing Data..	10		7		3		10

TABLE 7

PRIME OCCUPATION

Category	......Continent...... Africa	S.E. Asia	..Former Col. Power.. Britain	France	..First or 73 Leader.. First/58	Dec. 73	All Leaders Totals
Military.........	25 (29.4)	9 (31.0)	10 (28.6)	17 (34.0)	1 (3.8)	19 (73.1)	34 (29.8)
Education.......	17 (20.0)	2 (6.9)	6 (17.1)	11 (22.0)	7 (26.9)	1 (3.8)	19 (16.7)
Law............	6 (7.1)	7 (24.1)	7 (20.0)	1 (2.0)	3 (11.5)	3 (11.5)	13 (11.4)
Medical........	7 (8.2)	1 (3.4)	3 (8.6)	4 (8.0)	1 (3.8)	0 (0.0)	8 (7.0)
Other Pro- fessional......	2 (2.4)	0 (0.0)	0 (0.0)	2 (4.0)	1 (3.8)	0 (0.0)	2 (1.8)
Civil Service..	9 (10.6)	2 (6.9)	0 (0.0)	5 (10.0)	5 (19.2)	2 (7.7)	11 (9.6)
Commercial/ Business.......	6 (7.1)	1 (3.4)	2 (5.7)	3 (6.0)	3 (11.5)	1 (3.8)	7 (6.1)
Politician.....	3 (3.5)	3 (10.3)	4 (11.4)	2 (4.0)	2 (7.7)	0 (0.0)	6 (5.3)
Trad. Ruler....	4 (4.7)	1 (3.4)	2 (5.7)	1 (2.0)	2 (7.7)	0 (0.0)	5 (4.4)
Technical/ Engineer......	2 (2.4)	2 (6.9)	0 (0.0)	3 (6.0)	1 (3.8)	0 (0.0)	4 (3.5)
Agricultural...	1 (1.2)	0 (0.0)	1 (2.9)	0 (0.0)	0 (0.0)	0 (0.0)	1 (0.9)
Unknown........	3 (3.5)	1 (3.4)	0 (0.0)	1 (2.0)	0 (0.0)	0 (0.0)	4 (3.5)
Totals.....	85	29	35	50	26	26	114

Measures
	Continent	Former Col. Power	First or 73 Leader
Cramer's V...	.358	.485	.759
Cont. Coef...	.337	.436	.605
Cbar........	.426	.551	.764
Missing Data.	1		

TABLE 8

FIRST POLITICAL OR GOVERNMENTAL POSITION

| Category | ......Continent...... | | ..Former Col. Power.. | | ..First or 73 Leader.. | | All Leaders |
	Africa	S.E. Asia	Britain	France	First/58	Dec. 73	Totals
Party Post.....	10 (15.2)	6 (24.0)	4 (14.8)	9 (22.0)	8 (34.8)	2 (9.1)	16 (17.6)
Civil Service..	15 (22.7)	6 (24.0)	6 (22.2)	8 (19.5)	6 (26.1)	3 (13.6)	21 (23.1)
Elected Post...	13 (19.7)	1 (4.0)	2 (7.4)	9 (22.0)	5 (21.7)	2 (9.1)	14 (15.4)
Appt. Post.....	4 (6.1)	4 (16.0)	2 (7.4)	2 (4.9)	1 (4.3)	1 (4.5)	8 (8.8)
Military.......	19 (28.8)	8 (32.0)	9 (33.3)	13 (31.7)	2 (8.7)	14 (63.6)	27 (29.7)
Trad. Ruler....	4 (6.1)	0 (0.0)	3 (11.1)	0 (0.0)	1 (4.3)	0 (0.0)	4 (4.4)
None..........	1 (1.5)	0 (0.0)	1 (3.7)	0 (0.0)	0 (0.0)	0 (0.0)	1 (1.1)
Totals.....	66	24	27	41	23	22	90
Measures							
Cramer's V..	.291		.332		.594		
Cont. Coef...	.280		.315		.510		
Cbar........	.361		.407		.659		
Missing Data.	24		17		6		25

TABLE 9

AGE UPON ASSUMING FIRST PUBLIC POSITION, NON-MILITARY LEADERS

Category	Continent		Former Col. Power		First or 73 Leader		All Leaders Totals
	Africa	S.E. Asia	Britain	France	First/58	Dec. 73	
15-19	2 (4.0)	1 (6.7)	1 (5.0)	1 (3.6)	1 (4.2)	1 (16.7)	3 (4.6)
20-24	8 (16.0)	2 (13.3)	0 (0.0)	6 (21.4)	4 (16.7)	2 (33.3)	10 (15.4)
25-29	12 (24.0)	5 (33.3)	7 (35.0)	5 (17.9)	6 (25.0)	1 (16.7)	17 (26.2)
30-34	13 (26.0)	2 (13.3)	4 (20.0)	7 (25.0)	5 (20.8)	2 (33.3)	15 (23.1)
35-39	7 (14.0)	3 (20.0)	3 (15.0)	4 (14.3)	4 (16.7)	0 (0.0)	10 (15.4)
40-44	4 (8.0)	0 (0.0)	1 (5.0)	3 (10.7)	3 (12.5)	0 (0.0)	4 (6.2)
45-49	1 (2.0)	1 (6.7)	1 (5.0)	1 (3.6)	1 (4.2)	0 (0.0)	2 (3.1)
50-54	2 (4.0)	1 (6.7)	2 (10.0)	1 (3.6)	0 (0.0)	0 (0.0)	3 (4.6)
55 and over	1 (2.0)	0 (0.0)	1 (5.0)	0 (0.0)	0 (0.0)	0 (0.0)	1 (1.5)
Totals.....	50	15	20	28	24	6	65
Measures							
Cramer's V...	.254		.422		.377		
Cont. Coef...	.246		.388		.352		
Cbar........	.314		.496		.450		
Missing Data.	15		10		2		15

TABLE 10

POLITICAL PARTY EXPERIENCE OF NON-MILITARY LEADERS

| Category | ......Continent...... | | ..Former Col. Power.. | | ..First or 73 Leader.. | | All Leaders |
	Africa	S.E. Asia	Britain	France	First/58	Dec. 73	Totals
None.........	4 (9.1)	2 (12.5)	1 (5.3)	2 (8.0)	1 (4.5)	2 (28.6)	6 (10.2)
Under 1 year..	0 (0.0)	0 (0.0)	0 (0.0)	0 (0.0)	0 (0.0)	0 (0.0)	0 (0.0)
1-2 years.....	7 (15.9)	1 (6.3)	1 (5.3)	3 (12.0)	3 (13.6)	0 (0.0)	8 (13.6)
3-5 years.....	7 (15.9)	1 (6.3)	3 (15.8)	4 (16.0)	2 (9.1)	0 (0.0)	8 (13.6)
6 years and over.........	26 (59.1)	17 (75.0)	14 (73.7)	16 (64.0)	16 (72.7)	5 (71.4)	37 (62.7)
Totals......	44	16	19	25	22	7	59

Measures

Cramer's V...	.193		.135		.396		
Cont. Coef...	.190		.134		.368		
Cbar.........	.252		.178		.489		
Missing Data.	20		14		3		20

TABLE 11

LEGISLATIVE EXPERIENCE OF NON-MILITARY LEADERS

| Category | ......Continent...... | | ..Former Col. Power.. | | ..First or 73 Leader.. | | All Leaders |
	Africa	S.E. Asia	Britain	France	First/58	Dec. 73	Totals
None.........	8 (17.4)	3 (20.0)	3 (15.8)	5 (18.5)	7 (31.8)	1 (16.7)	11 (18.0)
Under 1 year..	5 (10.9)	0 (0.0)	1 (5.3)	2 (7.4)	3 (13.6)	0 (0.0)	5 (8.2)
1-2 years.....	7 (15.2)	2 (13.3)	5 (26.3)	3 (11.1)	1 (4.5)	1 (16.7)	9 (14.8)
3-5 years.....	11 (23.9)	1 (6.7)	3 (15.8)	8 (29.6)	5 (22.7)	0 (0.0)	12 (19.7)
6 years and over.........	15 (32.6)	9 (60.0)	7 (36.8)	9 (33.3)	6 (27.3)	4 (66.7)	24 (39.3)
Totals......	46	14	19	27	22	6	61

Measures

Cramer's V..	.302		.235		.446		
Cont. Coef..	.289		.229		.408		
Cbar........	.385		.305		.543		
Missing Data.	19		12		4		19

TABLE 12

CABINET EXPERIENCE OF NON-MILITARY LEADERS

Category	....Continent.... Africa	S.E. Asia	..Former Col. Power.. Britain	France	..First or 73 Leader.. First/58	Dec. 73	All Leaders Totals
None......	16 (35.6)	6 (33.3)	7 (36.8)	6 (21.4)	12 (52.2)	3 (42.9)	22 (34.9)
Under 1 year...	2 (4.4)	2 (11.1)	0 (0.0)	2 (7.1)	1 (4.3)	0 (0.0)	4 (6.3)
1-2 years......	10 (22.2)	4 (22.2)	5 (26.3)	8 (28.6)	5 (21.7)	0 (0.0)	14 (22.2)
3-5 years......	8 (17.8)	2 (11.1)	3 (15.8)	5 (17.9)	3 (13.0)	1 (14.3)	10 (15.9)
6 years and over......	9 (20.0)	4 (22.2)	4 (21.1)	7 (25.0)	2 (8.7)	3 (42.9)	13 (20.6)
Totals......	45	18	19	28	23	7	63
Measures							
Cramer's V...	.144		.229		.435		
Cont. Coef...	.143		.223		.399		
Cbar........	.192		.297		.531		
Missing Data.	17		11		2		17

TABLE 13

AGE WHEN FIRST BECAME CHIEF EXECUTIVE

Category	....Continent.... Africa	S.E. Asia	..Former Col. Power.. Britain	France	..First or 73 Leader.. First/58	Dec. 73	All Leaders Totals
10-19......	0 (0.0)	1 (3.4)	0 (0.0)	1 (2.2)	1 (4.0)	0 (0.0)	1 (0.9)
20-29......	3 (3.8)	0 (0.0)	0 (0.0)	0 (0.0)	0 (0.0)	2 (8.0)	3 (2.8)
30-39......	25 (31.3)	4 (13.8)	8 (22.9)	14 (30.4)	5 (20.0)	7 (28.0)	29 (26.6)
40-49......	24 (30.0)	10 (34.5)	12 (34.3)	11 (23.9)	10 (40.0)	8 (32.0)	34 (31.1)
50-59......	22 (27.5)	9 (31.0)	10 (28.6)	16 (34.8)	7 (28.0)	4 (16.0)	31 (28.4)
60-69......	5 (6.3)	4 (13.8)	4 (11.4)	3 (6.5)	2 (8.0)	4 (16.0)	9 (8.3)
70 and over...	1 (1.3)	1 (3.4)	1 (2.9)	1 (2.2)	0 (0.0)	0 (0.0)	2 (1.8)
Totals......	80	29	35	46	25	25	109
Measures							
Cramer's V...	.280		.185		.318		
Cont. Coef...	.270		.182		.303		
Cbar........	.349		.235		.419		
Missing Data.	6		4		1		6

TABLE 14

MEANS OF ASSUMING POWER

| Category | ......Continent...... | | ..Former Col. Power.. | | ..First or 73 Leader.. | | All Leaders Totals |
	Africa	S.E. Asia	Britain	France	First/58	Dec. 73	
Const. Transfer	52 (62.7)	16 (59.3)	23 (65.7)	24 (52.2)	22 (91.7)	7 (26.9)	68 (59.1)
Military Coup..	27 (32.5)	8 (29.6)	11 (31.4)	17 (37.0)	1 (4.2)	17 (65.4)	35 (36.4)
Other Coup.....	3 (3.6)	2 (7.4)	1 (2.9)	4 (8.7)	0 (0.0)	2 (7.7)	5 (4.3)
Hereditary.....	1 (1.2)	1 (3.7)	0 (0.0)	1 (2.2)	1 (4.2)	0 (0.0)	2 (1.7)
Totals.....	83	27	35	46	25	26	110
Measures							
Cramer's V...	.114		.181		.706		
Cont. Coef...	.114		.178		.577		
Cbar.........	.156		.244		.790		
Missing Data.	5		4		1		5

TABLE 15

AVERAGE TENURE OF CHIEF EXECUTIVES
(1958 or Independence/# of Chief Executives)

	Average Period Since 1958 or Indep. to Dec. 31, 1973	No. of Leaders	Average Tenure
All Countries (45)	12 yrs., 9 mos.	115	5 yrs., 1 mo.
By Continent			
S.E. Asia (10)	14 yrs., 8 mos.	30	5 yrs., 1 mo.
Africa (35)	12 yrs., 3 mos.	85	5 yrs., 1 mo.
By Colonial Power:			
Former French (19)	14 yrs., 1 mo.	50	5 yrs., 4 mos.
Former British (10)	10 yrs., 9 mos.	35	4 yrs., 11 mos.

CHART A

DISTRIBUTION OF CHIEF EXECUTIVES BY TOTAL TIME SERVED

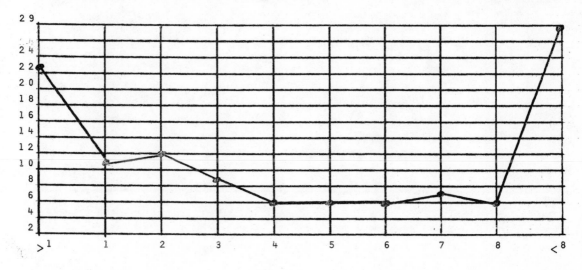

AFRICA PROGRAM
CENTER FOR INTERNATIONAL
  STUDIES
OHIO UNIVERSITY
ATHENS, OHIO 45701

ORDER FROM:
  Ohio University Press
  Administrative Annex
  Ohio University
  Athens, Ohio 45701

*Publication
Number:*

1 - THE NEW ENGLISH OF THE ONITSHA CHAPBOOKS. By Harold Reeves Collins. Pp. v, 17. 1968. $1.75

2 - DIRECTIONS IN GHANAIAN LINGUISTICS: A Brief Survey. By Paul F.A. Kotey. Pp. v, 15. 1969. $1.75

3 - DEFINING NATIONAL PURPOSE IN LESOTHO. By Richard F. Weisfelder. Pp. xi, 28. 1969. $2.25

4 - RECENT AGRICULTURAL CHANGE EAST OF MOUNT KENYA. By Frank E. Bernard. Pp. v, 36. 1969. $2.75

5 - THE STRUGGLE AGAINST SLEEPING SICKNESS IN NYASALAND AND NORTHERN RHODESIA, 1900-1922. By Norman H. Pollock. Pp. v, 16. 1969. $1.75

6 - BOTSWANA AND ITS SOUTHERN NEIGHBOR: The Patterns of Linkage and the Options in Statecraft. By Richard Dale. *Out of print.*

7 - WOLF COURTS GIRL: The Equivalence of Hunting and Mating in Bushman Thought. By Daniel F. McCall. Pp. v, 19. 1970. $1.75

8 - MARKERS IN ENGLISH-INFLUENCED SWAHILI CONVERSATION. By Carol M. Eastman. Pp. v, 20. 1970. $2.00

9 - THE TERRITORIAL EXPANSION OF THE NANDI OF KENYA, 1500-1905. By Bob J. Walter. Pp. vii, 30. 1970. $3.00

10 - SOME GEOGRAPHICAL ASPECTS OF WEST AFRICAN DEVELOPMENT. By R.J. Harrison Church. Pp. v, 29. 1970. $2.75

11 - THE IMPACT OF THE PROTÉGÉ SYSTEM IN MOROCCO, 1800-1912. By Leland Bowie. Pp. vi, 16. 1970. $1.75

12 - MARKET DEVELOPMENT IN TRADITIONALLY MARKETLESS SOCIETIES: A Perspective on East Africa. By Charles M. Good. Pp. vi, 34. 1971. $3.00

13 - SOUTH AFRICA'S OUTWARD STRATEGY: A Foreign Policy Dilemma for the United States. By Larry W. Bowman. Pp. vii, 25. 1971. $2.50

14 - BANTU EDUCATION AND THE EDUCATION OF AFRICANS IN SOUTH AFRICA. By R. Hunt Davis, Jr. Pp. vii, 53. 1972. $3.50

15 - TOWARD A THEORY OF THE AFRICAN UPPER STRATUM IN SOUTH AFRICA. By Thomas E. Nyquist. Pp. vii, 56. 1972. $3.50

16 - THE BASOTHO MONARCHY: A Spent Force or a Dynamic Political Factor? By Richard F. Weisfelder. Pp. ix, 97. 1972. $4.00

17 - YORUBA PROVERBS: Translation and Annotation. By Bernth Lindfors and Oyekan Owomoyela. Pp. ix, 82. 1973. $4.00

18 - POST-MILITARY COUP STRATEGY IN UGANDA: Amin's Early Attempts to Consolidate Political Support. By Jeffrey T. Strate. Pp. vii, 70. 1973. $3.75

19 - HIGHLAND MOSAIC: A Critical Anthology of Ethiopian Literature in English. Compiled by Paul E. Huntsberger. Pp. ix, 122. 1973. $4.75

20 - THE KENYA NATIONAL YOUTH SERVICE: A Governmental Response to Young Political Activists. By Richard L. Coe. Pp. vi, 33. 1973. $2.50

21 - CONSTRAINTS ON THE EXPANSION OF COMMERCIAL AGRICULTURE: Iringa District, Tanzania. By Marilyn Silberfein. Pp. vii, 51. 1974. $3.50

22 - ECHO AND CHORUSES: "Ballad of the Cells" and Selected Shorter Poems. By Cosmo Pieterse. Pp. ix, 66. 1974. $3.75

23 - THE NIGER-NIGERIAN BOUNDARY, 1890-1906: A Study of Ethnic Frontiers and a Colonial Boundary. By Derrick J. Thom. Pp. vii, 42. 1975. $3.25

24 - A COMPREHENSIVE PERIODICAL BIBLIOGRAPHY OF NIGERIA, 1960-1970. Compiled by Edward Baum. Pp. xii, 249. 1975. $6.00

25 - ABYSSINIA TO ZONA AL SUR DEL DRAA: A Guide to the Political Units of Africa in the Period 1950-1974. Second Edition. By Eugene C. Kirchherr. Pp. x, 40. 1975. $3.50

26 - THE ORIGINS AND DEVELOPMENT OF EFIK SETTLEMENTS IN SOUTHEASTERN NIGERIA. By Kannan K. Nair. Pp. vi, 36. 1975. $3.00

27 - MOUNTAIN WARRIORS: The Pre-Colonial Meru of Mt. Kenya. By Jeffrey Fadiman. Pp. vii, 75, Bibliography. 1976. $4.00

28 - DEPENDENCE AND UNDERDEVELOPMENT: The Development and Foreign Policies of Zambia. By Timothy M. Shaw. Pp. vii, 60, Bibliography. 1976. $3.75

29 - CHIEF EXECUTIVES IN BLACK AFRICA AND SOUTHEAST ASIA: A Descriptive Analysis of Social Background   Characteristics. By Edward Baum and Felix Gagliano. Pp. viii, 35, Appendix A and B. 1976. $3.00

ALSO: WEST/AFRICAN PIDGIN-ENGLISH: A Descriptive Linguistic Analysis with Texts and Glossary from the Cameroon Area. By Gilbert D. Schneider. Pp. xiv, 242. 1969. $6.00

This book is an attempt to apply the basic principles of structural linguistics to West African Pidgin-English. After an introductory chapter which deals with the general characteristics of the language as spoken in the Cameroon area, the author proceeds to the treatment of sounds, meaningful units, and sentence patterns. A glossary and bibliography are included.

SOUTHEAST ASIA PROGRAM
CENTER FOR INTERNATIONAL
  STUDIES
OHIO UNIVERSITY
ATHENS, OHIO 45701

ORDER FROM:
  Ohio University
  Administrative Annex
  Ohio University
  Athens, Ohio 45701

*Publication
Number:*

1 - TREASURES AND TRIVIA: Doctoral Dissertations on Southeast
    Asia Accepted by Universities in the United States. Com-
    piled by Lian The and Paul W. van der Veur. Pp. xiv, 141,
    Appendix, Index. 1968. $5.00

2 - PUBLIC PROTEST IN INDONESIA. By Ann Ruth Willner. Pp. vii,
    14. 1968. $1.75

3 - DEVELOPMENTAL CHALLENGE IN MALAYSIA. By Siew Nim Chee. Pp.
    v, 17. 1968. $1.75

4 - THE USE OF HISTORY. By Wang Gungwu. Pp. vii, 17. 1968. $1.75

5 - THE TRADITIONAL USE OF THE FORESTS IN MAINLAND SOUTHEAST
    ASIA. By James L. Cobban. *Out of print.*

6 - CONFLICT AND POLITICAL DEVELOPMENT IN SOUTHEAST ASIA: An
    Exploration in the International Implications of Compara-
    tive Theory. By Gerald S. Maryanov. *Out of print.*

7 - SRI PADUKA: The Exile of the Prince of Ayodhya. Translated
    by S.M. Ponniah. *Out of print.*

8 - AGRARIAN UNREST IN THE PHILIPPINES: Guardia de Honor --
    Revitalization within the Revolution; Rizalistas -- Con-
    temporary Revitalization Movements in the Philippines.
    By David R. Sturtevant. Pp. vii, 30. 1969. $2.75

9 - PANDANGGO-SA-ILAW: The Politics of Occidental Mindoro.
    By Remigio E. Agpalo. Pp. ix, 23. 1969. $2.00

10 - REPRESSION AND REVOLT: The Origins of the 1948 Communist
     Insurrection in Malaya and Singapore. By Michael R.
     Stenson. *Out of print.*

11 - RUBBER AND THE MALAYSIAN ECONOMY: Implications of Declin-
     ing Prices. By Tan Sri Lim Swee Aun. Pp. v, 31. 1969. $2.50

12 - EDUCATION AND SOCIAL CHANGE IN COLONIAL INDONESIA: I.
     Progress and Procrastination in Education in Indonesia prior
     to World War II; II. The Social and Geographical Origins
     of Dutch-Educated Indonesians. By Paul W. van der Veur.
     Pp. xiii, 49. 1969. $3.50

13 - COMMUNAL VIOLENCE IN MALAYSIA 1969: The Political Aftermath.
     By Felix V. Gagliano. *Out of print.*

14 - SOVIET AND AMERICAN AID TO INDONESIA 1949-1968. By Usha
     Mahajani. *Out of print.*

15 - POLITICS AMONG BURMANS: A Study of Intermediary Leaders.
     By John Badgley. Pp. x, 115. 1970. $4.50

16 - TRADE AND EMPIRE IN MALAYA AND SINGAPORE, 1869-1874. By
     D. R. SarDesai. Pp. v, 17. 1970. $1.75

*Publication
Number:*

17 - EXPANSION OF THE VIETNAM WAR INTO CAMBODIA: Action and Response by the Governments of North Vietnam, South Vietnam, Cambodia, and the United States. By Peter A. Poole. Pp. xi, 59. 1970. $3.50

18 - THE PRE-WORLD WAR II PERANAKAN CHINESE PRESS OF JAVA: A Preliminary Survey. By Leo Suryadinata. Pp. ix, 35. 1971. $2.75

19 - A REVIEW OF COMMUNITY-ORIENTED ECOLOGICAL RESEARCH IN THE PHILIPPINES. By Robert A. Bullington. *Out of print.*

20 - A BIBLIOGRAPHY OF PHILIPPINE LINGUISTICS. By Nobleza C. Asuncion-Landé. *Out of print.*

21 - THE BURMA-YUNNAN RAILWAY: Anglo-French Rivalry in Mainland Southeast Asia and South China, 1895-1902. By J. Chandran. *Out of print.*

22 - THE NORTH BORNEO CHARTERED COMPANY'S ADMINISTRATION OF THE BAJAU, 1878-1909: The Pacification of a Maritime, Nomadic People. By James F. Warren. *Out of print.*

23 - PROMINENT INDONESIAN CHINESE IN THE TWENTIETH CENTURY: A Preliminary Survey. By Leo Suryadinata. *Out of print.*

24 - PEACOCKS, PAGODAS, AND PROFESSOR HALL: A Critique of the Persisting Use of Historiography as an Apology for British Empire-Building in Burma. By Manuel Sarkisyanz. Pp. xi, 57. 1972. $3.50

25 - IMBALANCES IN DEVELOPMENT: The Indonesian Experience. By Selo Soemardjan. Pp. v, 21. 1972. $2.00

26 - THE VERHANDELINGEN VAN HET BATAVIAASCH GENOOTSCHAP: An Annotated Content Analysis. Compiled by Lian The and Paul W. van der Veur. Pp. xi, 140, Index. 1973. $5.00

27 - JAPAN'S SCHEME FOR THE LIBERATION OF BURMA: The Role of the Minami Kikan and the "Thirty Comrades." by Won Z. Yoon. Pp. xi, 54, Bibliography. 1973. $3.50

28 - EDUCATIONAL SPONSORSHIP BY ETHNICITY: A Preliminary Analysis of the West Malaysian Experience. By Yoshimitsu Takei, John C. Bock, and Bruce Saunders. Pp. vii, 37. 1973. $3.00

29 - BLOOD, BELIEVER, AND BROTHER: The Development of Voluntary Associations in Malaysia. By Stephen A. Douglas and Paul Pedersen. Pp. viii, 111, Appendix. 1973. $4.50

30 - THE DYNAMICS OF POLITICS AND ADMINISTRATION IN RURAL THAILAND. By Clark D. Neher. *Out of print.*

31 - PEASANT CITIZENS: Politics, Religion, and Modernization in Kelantan, Malaysia. By Manning Nash. *Out of print.*

32 - MARGINAL MAN IN A COLONIAL SOCIETY: Abdoel Moeis' *Salah Asuhan.* By David de Queljoe. Pp. v, 38. 1974. $3.00

Publication
Number:

33 - THE NEUTRALIZATION OF SOUTHEAST ASIA: An Analysis of the
Malaysian/ASEAN Proposal. By Marvin C. Ott. Pp. vii, 50.
1974. $3.50

34 - THE LAND-TO-THE-TILLER PROGRAM AND RURAL RESOURCE
MOBILIZATION IN THE MEKONG DELTA OF SOUTH VIETNAM. By
C. Stuart Callison. Pp. vi, 41. 1974. $3.00

35 - THE FUTURE OF BURMA IN PERSPECTIVE: A Symposium. Edited
and with an Introduction by Josef Silverstein. Pp. xi,
100. 1974. $4.00

36 - INDOCHINA: PERSPECTIVES FOR RECONCILIATION. Edited and
with an Introduction by Peter A. Poole. Pp. vii, 84.
1975. $4.25

37 - THE COMINTERN AND VIETNAMESE COMMUNISM. By William J.
Duiker. Pp. vi, 42. 1975. $3.25

38 - BROKER, MEDIATOR, PATRON AND KINSMAN: Key Leadership
Roles in a Rural Malaysian District. By Connor Bailey.
Pp. x, 79, Bibliography. 1976. LC75-620141. $4.25

39 - CHIEF EXECUTIVES IN BLACK AFRICA AND SOUTHEAST ASIA:
A Descriptive Analysis of Social Background and
Characteristics. By Edward Baum and Felix Gagliano.
Pp. viii, 35, Appendix A and B. 1976. $3.00

ALSO: INTERNATIONAL BIOGRAPHICAL DIRECTORY OF SOUTHEAST ASIA
SPECIALISTS. Compiled by Robert O. Tilman. Pp. xxxv,
337. 1969. Special price: $1.25

A collection of about 1,000 vitae of Southeast Asia
specialists throughout the world preceded by an introductory analysis of the data collected. The study was
undertaken as a project by the Inter-University
Southeast Asia Committee of the Association for Asian
Studies.